Water

Edited by Rebecca Stefoff

Text © 1990 by Garrett Educational Corporation
First Published in the United States in 1990 by Garrett Educational
Corporation, 130 E. 13th Street, Ada, OK74820

First Published 1988 by A&C Black (Publishers) Limited, London with
the title WATER © 1988 A&C Black (Publishers) Ltd.

All rights reserved including the right of reproduction in whole or in part
in any form without the prior written permission of the publisher.
Published by Garrett Educational Corporation, 130 East 13th Street, Ada,
Oklahoma 74820

Manufactured in the United States of America.

Library of Congress Cataloging-in-Publication Data

Walpole, Brenda.
    Water / Brenda Walpole ; photographs by Ed Barber.
    p.   cm. - (Threads)
    Includes index.
    Summary: Explains the many uses of water and how clean water gets
to the household tap. Includes instructions for a variety of simple experiments.
    ISBN 0-944483-72-0
    1. Water- Experiments-Juvenile literature. [1. Water. 2. Water-
Experiments. 3. Experiments.] I. Barber, Ed, ill. II. Title. III. Series.
GB662.3.W35   1990
546'.22-dc20

                                                    90-40381
                                                      CIP
                                                      AC
                                                      Rev.

Water

Brenda Walpole

Photographs by Ed Barber

Atlanta-Jackson Twp. Public Library
Atlanta, IN 46031

3-94 Garrett 11.35 94-333

Contents

GEC GARRETT EDUCATIONAL CORPORATION

What is water like?

It has no taste.

It fits into all sorts of shapes.

Most of the water you use is a liquid. Liquid water has no shape of its own. Can you draw the shape of frozen water or boiling water?

When you are thirsty, water is refreshing, but it doesn't have much flavor or smell.

Put your hand into some water. What does it feel like? Does the water make your hand look different?

Fill a large bowl or tank with water and collect some different objects to put into the water.

Before you put each object into the water, guess whether it will float or sink. Did you guess correctly?

What do you use water for?

Look at this picture and see if you can spot the different ways in which children are using water. *(The answers are on page 25.)*

4

You also use water in lots of other ways.

To flush the toilet

To wash yourself

and your clothes

For cooking

To keep you warm

Can you think of some more ways that you use water at home or at school?

5

Water for special occasions

Water is so important to us that it is often used on special occasions.

Christians have a ceremony called baptism to mark the time when a person begins a new life as a Christian. People are often baptized when they are babies. The minister or priest sprinkles holy water over the baby's head to baptize the baby.

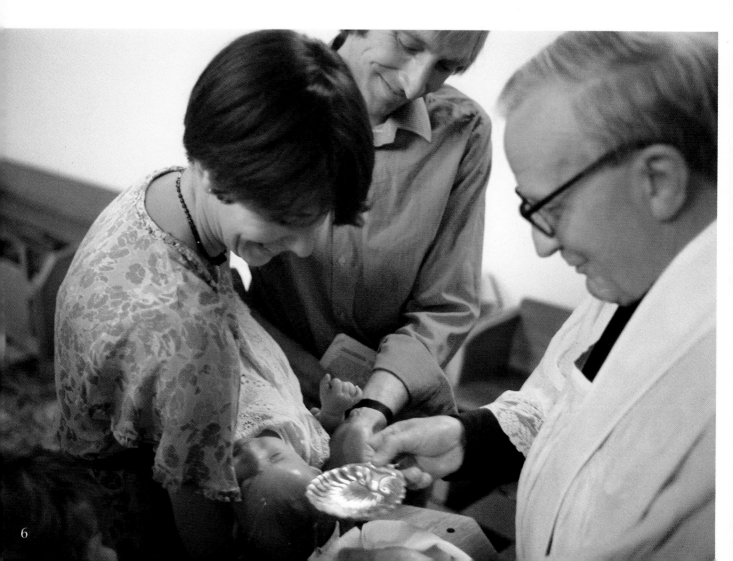

Muslims wash in a special way before they say their
prayers. They believe they should be especially clean
before they pray to God.

At the entrance to a mosque, which is what Muslims call
their place of worship, there is always a water faucet or a
pool of water that people use for washing. The pool in the
picture is outside a big mosque in Delhi, India.

Can you think of any other special occasions where water
is important?

Water inside you

Did you know that most of you is water? About two-thirds of your body is water, and water is in every part of you. Without water, you could not live for more than a few days.

Every day you lose a lot of water when you sweat and go to the bathroom. Each time you breathe out, a tiny bit of water goes out with the air. You can see the water in your breath if you say "haaaaa" onto a mirror.

If you don't replace all the water you lose each day, you may become ill. To stay healthy, you need to drink about six large glasses of water a day. Don't forget that milk, juice, tea, soup, and canned drinks are made mostly of water.

The water can be taken out of some foods so they will keep for a long time without going "bad" or turning moldy. What happens when you soak dried peas in water?

Make a note of how long you leave the peas to soak. Compare the size and weight of the peas before and after you soak them. What has happened?

You also eat a lot of water. You can't always see the water by looking at food from the outside. Cut up an orange and squeeze all the pieces into a glass. How much juice comes out?

The juice is mostly water, but it contains sugar and vitamins, too. Does a melon or a cucumber contain more water than an orange?

Where does water come from?

Most of the water we use comes from the rain that falls from the sky. The rain collects in puddles, lakes, ponds, and streams. Small streams join together to make large rivers that flow into the ocean. When it stops raining, the puddles seem to disappear. Where does the water go?

The heat of the sun turns the water into an invisible mist called water vapor. The water vapor rises into the sky. This is called evaporation.

High in the sky, the air is cold. The cold air makes the water vapor turn into drops of water, which collect together to make a cloud.

The drops of water join together and grow bigger. When they become too heavy to hang in the sky, they fall to the ground as rain.

Try this test to find out why the water in some puddles evaporates faster than in others.

You will need

Some water

A pen

Two saucers

A measuring cup

How to do it

Fill each saucer with the same amount of water. Use the pen to mark the level of water. Leave one saucer in a warm place and put the other saucer in a cool place.

After a few hours, which saucer has more water in it?

Try the same test outside on a windy day. Put both saucers in the sun, but put one in a sheltered spot and leave one where the wind will blow on it. Which saucer has more water left in it this time? What sort of weather do you think would be best for drying the wash?

Most of our drinking water comes from rivers and wells. This water has trickled through soil and rocks. Leaves and grass have fallen into it, animals and plants have lived and died in it, and people have dumped garbage into it.

This water is dirty and full of germs. If you drink water like this, it will make you ill. The water from rivers and wells has to be cleaned at a waterworks to make it safe for us to drink.

To see how this is done, try cleaning some dirty water. First you will need to make a mixture of muddy water.

You will need

Leaves and twigs

Pieces of chalk

A large bowl

Water   Small stones   Sand

Some soil   An old spoon

Put everything into the bowl and stir it around with the old spoon. (Keep this muddy water; you will find out how to clean it later.)

At the waterworks

At this waterworks, the water from a river goes through thick metal bars that trap large objects, such as leaves and branches.

Then the water is pumped to a reservoir. Here most of the water does not move, so some of the dirt, stones, and larger objects sink to the bottom. If you let your bowl of muddy water stand for a few days, you will see this happening.

Turn the page to see where the water goes next.

13

From the reservoir, the water is pumped to the strainer building. Here there are lots of steel drums that turn around and around very slowly. Can you see the holes in this drum?

The water goes into the middle of each drum and comes out through holes in the sides. Pieces of dirt and tiny water plants called algae are trapped inside the drum.

You can try straining your muddy water through a strainer. Does this make the water look cleaner?

Even though the water is cleaner when it comes out of the strainers, it is still not clean enough for you to drink. Next, it has to be filtered. You can make your own filter to see how this works.

How to make a water filter

You will need

A plastic flowerpot with holes in the bottom (a 6-inch pot is about right)

Gravel or small stones

Blotting paper or coffee filter paper liners

Coarse, damp sand

Muddy water (see page 12)

Layer your filter so it looks like this.

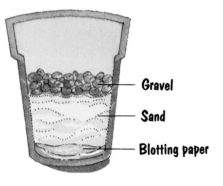

Gravel

Sand

Blotting paper

How to use your filter

Put a bowl underneath the flowerpot and pour the muddy water slowly through the filter. You may need to ask a friend to help you.

Some of the dirt will stick to the sand and gravel, so the water will look a bit cleaner when it comes out of the bottom of the filter. But your filtered water will still be dirty, and there will be germs in it. The germs are too small to see. Don't drink this water.

The filters at a waterworks are at least ten times thicker than your filter. They get the water much cleaner than your flowerpot filter.

Turn the page to find out how these filters work.

15

Each filter bed is a big concrete tank that looks a bit like a swimming pool. On the bottom of the filter bed is a layer of gravel, and on top of the gravel is a layer of sand.

Sand

Gravel

Tiny pieces of dirt are trapped by the sand and gravel, just as they were in your flowerpot filter. When the sand gets very dirty, the top layer has to be scraped off and washed.

The cleaned water flows out through pipes at the bottom of each filter bed.

It goes to another building where a small amount of chlorine is added to kill any germs left in the water.

When the water comes out of the chlorine building, it is ready to be pumped to houses and factories. In the picture, you can see some of the pumping machines.

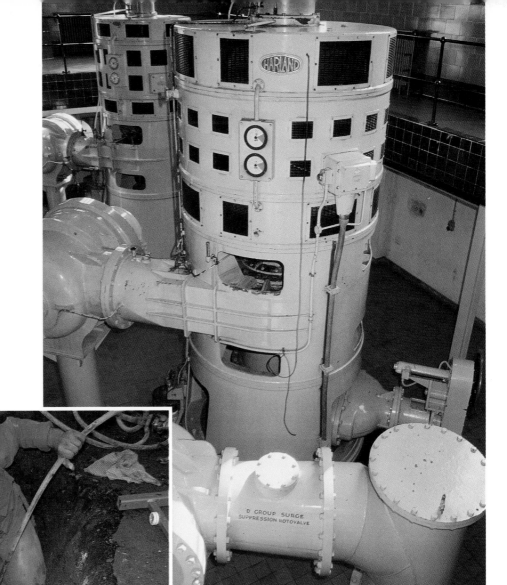

The water travels along pipes that are buried underground. The largest pipes are as wide as the trunk of a big tree. They are called water mains.

You may see the water mains when workers are digging up a street.

Water from your faucet

Small pipes carry clean water from the road to the faucets and water tanks inside houses and other buildings. When you turn on the faucet, pure, clean water comes out.

Even though tap water is clean enough for drinking and washing, it has tiny amounts of mineral salts dissolved in it.

These minerals get into rainwater when it trickles through rocks such as limestone. The minerals don't do us any harm.

Water that contains a lot of minerals is called "hard" water. Water that contains a small amount of minerals is called "soft" water.

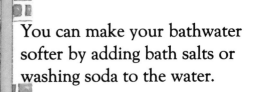

You can make your bathwater softer by adding bath salts or washing soda to the water.

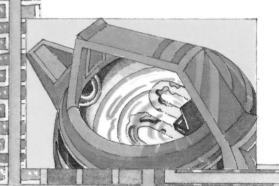

If your teapot has a whitish or yellowish crust inside, it comes from the minerals in hard water.

When people use water, they make it dirty. Where does all this dirty water go?

Take a look outside your home or school. Can you see pipes coming out of the walls? The pipes go underground and join up with pipes from other houses. Dirty water from factories, offices, and paved areas also goes into underground pipes.

All these pipes go into larger pipes called sewers. The sewers take all the dirty water to the sewage treatment plant. The largest sewers are big enough for people to stand up in. These men are inspecting a sewer.

f you have hard water,
ou will have to use a lot of
oap to wash things.

At the sewage treatment plant

At the sewage treatment plant, dirty water is cleaned before it is put back into rivers and the sea.

1. When the sewage arrives at this treatment plant, it goes through large metal bars. Large objects, such as wood and plastic, get caught on the bars and are lifted out with rakes.

2. Next, the mucky liquid flows into large tanks like the one in this photograph. Because the water is moving slowly, small particles in the water sink to the bottom of the tank. They collect to make a slimy mud called sludge.

The sludge goes to large towers where bacteria destroy the smelly materials.

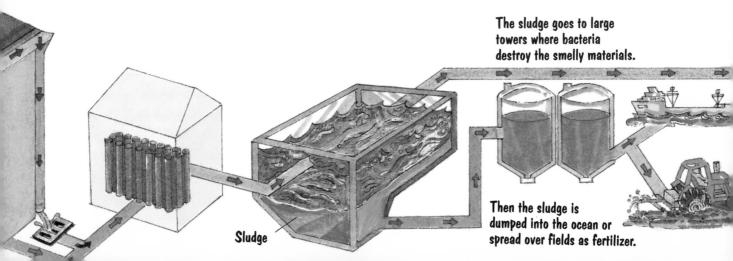

Sludge

Then the sludge is dumped into the ocean or spread over fields as fertilizer.

3. The dirty water from the top of the tanks goes into another tank. Here bacteria eat up harmful dirt and germs in the sewage.

The water from the bacteria tanks goes into some more tanks like these, where it is left to stand still.

4. The water from the top of these tanks is clean enough to go back into the river. Scientists test the water every day to make sure it does not contain harmful substances.

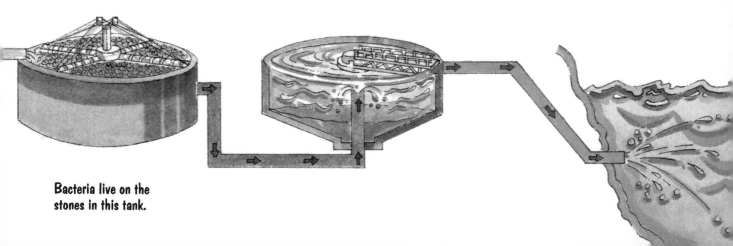

Bacteria live on the stones in this tank.

Water pollution

Even though most dirty water is cleaned at sewage treatment plants, harmful substances do sometimes get into rivers, lakes, and oceans. This makes the water polluted, so it is dangerous for people to use. Pollution also kills plants and animals that live in the water. Scientists take samples of water to check for signs of pollution.

Here are some of the things that can make water polluted.

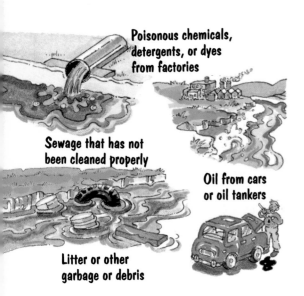

Poisonous chemicals, detergents, or dyes from factories

Sewage that has not been cleaned properly

Oil from cars or oil tankers

Litter or other garbage or debris

Make sure you don't leave any litter in or near a pond or river. You may also be able to help your teacher or a conservation group clean up a pond or river near your home or school.

Water for wildlife

If water is not polluted, lots of different plants and animals can live in or near the water. You may be able to study the wildlife in a pond or river. Always go with an adult—water can be dangerous. Remember to put the plants and animals back into the water as soon as possible.

23

How much water?

Whenever you need some water, you just turn on the faucet. There always seems to be plenty of clean water. But have you ever thought about how much water you use every day? Try and work it out for yourself. Here are some measurements to help you.

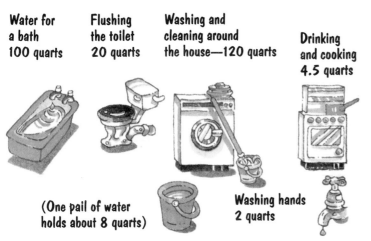

Water for a bath 100 quarts

Flushing the toilet 20 quarts

Washing and cleaning around the house—120 quarts

Drinking and cooking 4.5 quarts

(One pail of water holds about 8 quarts)

Washing hands 2 quarts

All these measurements are the average amount of water that one person uses in a day.

You can make a chart from your measurements.

In many parts of the world, there is not enough rain to provide this much water for everybody. Water has to be used very carefully so that people and crops have enough water to survive.

Now you know where water comes from and how it is cleaned before and after you use it. The next time you turn the faucet or drink some water, think about the long trip the water has taken before it reaches you.

More things to do

1. See if you can find out why boats float on the water. They must be very heavy, so why don't they sink?
Take two pieces of modeling clay. Make sure they are exactly the same size. Roll one piece into a ball and make the other piece into a boat shape. Put both pieces of clay into a bowl of water. What happens. How does the shape of a boat help it to float on water?

2. Try mixing different things with water. Here are some ideas: sand, salt, cooking oil, jelly, tea leaves, orange pulp, rice, powdered soup, ink. What happens? Does it make a difference if the water is warm?

3. The next time you go to the supermarket, see how many different kinds of mineral water you can find. Read the labels on the bottles and try to find out more about the minerals in the water.

4. Seeds must soak up water to help them sprout roots and leaves. Fill two flowerpots with soil and plant the same number of seeds in each pot. Watercress seeds are good ones to try. Leave both pots in a warm place. Give one pot enough water to keep the soil damp and don't water the other pot at all. Which seeds grow better?

5. Try making a magnifying glass from a drop of water. Find a small piece of thin cardboard and cut a hole about 3/4-inch wide in the middle. Stick a piece of clear tape across the hole and then put a drop or water on top. Look at this page through the drop of water. Does the water make the writing look bigger or smaller?

6. Some of the chemicals in the smoke from factory chimneys mix with rainwater to make acid rain. See if you can find out more about acid rain. How does it harm animals and plants?

Page 4—answer: Painting; marbling paper; watering plant; giving fish more water; measuring out tap water; doing experiments with floating, sinking, and capacity.

Index